Building Character

Resisting Bullying

by Rebecca Pettiford

Bullfrog Books

Ideas for Parents and Teachers

Bullfrog Books let children practice reading informational text at the earliest reading levels. Repetition, familiar words, and photo labels support early readers.

Before Reading

- Discuss the cover photo. What does it tell them?

- Look at the picture glossary together. Read and discuss the words.

Read the Book

- "Walk" through the book and look at the photos. Let the child ask questions. Point out the photo labels.

- Read the book to the child, or have him or her read independently.

After Reading

- Prompt the child to think more. Ask: Have you ever experienced or witnessed bullying? How did it make you feel?

Bullfrog Books are published by Jump!
5357 Penn Avenue South
Minneapolis, MN 55419
www.jumplibrary.com

Copyright © 2018 Jump! International copyright reserved in all countries. No part of this book may be reproduced in any form without written permission from the publisher.

Library of Congress Cataloging-in-Publication Data is available at www.loc.gov or upon request from the publisher.

ISBN: 978-1-62031-882-9 (hardcover)
ISBN: 978-1-62031-883-6 (paperback)
ISBN: 978-1-62496-645-3 (ebook)

Editor: Kirsten Chang
Book Designer: Michelle Sonnek
Photo Researchers: Michelle Sonnek & Kirsten Chang

Photo Credits: Sabphoto/Shutterstock, cover; Serhiy Kobyakov/Shutterstock, 1; Beth Swanson/Shutterstock, 3 (sign); KK Tan/Shutterstock, 3 (girl), 12, 23tr; wavebreakmedia/Shutterstock, 4, 6–7, 18–19; Suzanne Tucker/Shutterstock, 5; Image Source/Getty, 8, 23br; Gagliardilmages/Shutterstock, 9; Phanie/SuperStock, 10–11; Pandora Studio/Shutterstock, 12–13; Yellow Dog Productions/Getty, 14–15; karelnoppe/Shutterstock, 16, 23bl; Ianych/Shutterstock, 17; paulaphoto/Shutterstock, 20–21, 23tl; udovichenko/Shutterstock, 22 (background); Melissa King/Shutterstock, 22 (foreground); koTRA/Shutterstock, 24.

Printed in the United States of America at Corporate Graphics in North Mankato, Minnesota.

Table of Contents

No to Bullies!

Bullies hurt others.

They use mean words.
Some push and hit.

We stand up to bullies.

How? We say no.

We get help.

Jill teases Cam.
What does he do?

He walks away.

He finds his friends.

Carl pushes Bo.
What does he do?
He says, "No!"
He doesn't
push back.

A cyberbully calls
Mia names.

What does she do?

She tells her mom.

cyberbully

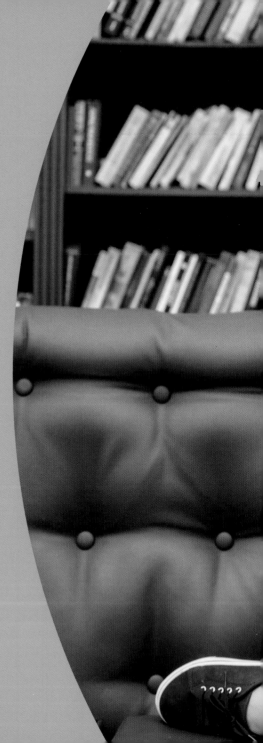

Bullies make fun
of Stan.

What does he do?

He asks an adult
for help.

A bully yells at Shay.
What does she do?

She says, "Stop!"
She walks away.

We never bully others.
We are kind to everyone.

Be a buddy, not a bully!

Help Stop Bullying

This book talks about five ways to stop bullies. They are:

1. Walk away.
2. Say, "no!" or "stop!"
3. Tell an adult or parent.
4. Ask for help.
5. Be a friend.

You can make a poster to remind you of the five ways you can stop bullying.

You will need:

- two sheets of colored construction paper (one light, one dark)
- pencil
- colored markers
- safety scissors
- glue or rubber cement

Directions:

❶ Use a pencil to draw an outline of your hand on the lighter sheet of paper.

❷ Write one way to stop bullying on each finger.

❸ Cut out your hand outline and glue it onto the darker sheet of paper.

❹ Hang the paper in your room so you can see it every day. It will help you remember how important it is to stop bullies. It will help you remember to be a friend.

Picture Glossary

buddy
A friend.

cyberbully
Someone who posts mean messages over a computer or phone.

bully
Someone who is mean to other people.

tease
To laugh at or be mean to someone.

Index

To Learn More

Learning more is as easy as 1, 2, 3.

1) Go to www.factsurfer.com

2) Enter "resistingbullying" into the search box.

3) Click the "Surf" button to see a list of websites.

With factsurfer.com, finding more information is just a click away.